AF479935

RED PANDA!

Fun Animal Facts for Kids with Real Photos

Dylanna Press

LEVEL 1

EARLY READER

Red Panda!
Fun Animal Facts for Kids with Real Photos
(Amazing Animals for Young Readers – Level 1)

Published by Dylanna Publishing, inc.
www.dylannapublishing.com

Cover design and layout by Julie Grady
Photo credits: All images licensed from Shutterstock

ISBN: 978-1-64790-490-6

This book is a work of nonfiction created for educational purposes. While efforts have been made to ensure accuracy, it is intended for early readers and may simplify or generalize information.

First edition, 2026

Meet the Red Panda

Hi there!

Look at this small, furry animal!

It's a red panda — and it's not actually a panda at all!

What Do They Look Like?

Red pandas have reddish fur and black legs. They have a white face — and that tail? Striped and bushy!

Masked Face
Peek-a-boo!
Red pandas have white eye patches. It looks like a little mask!

A red panda's tail has rings. Light stripes. Dark stripes. Over and over!

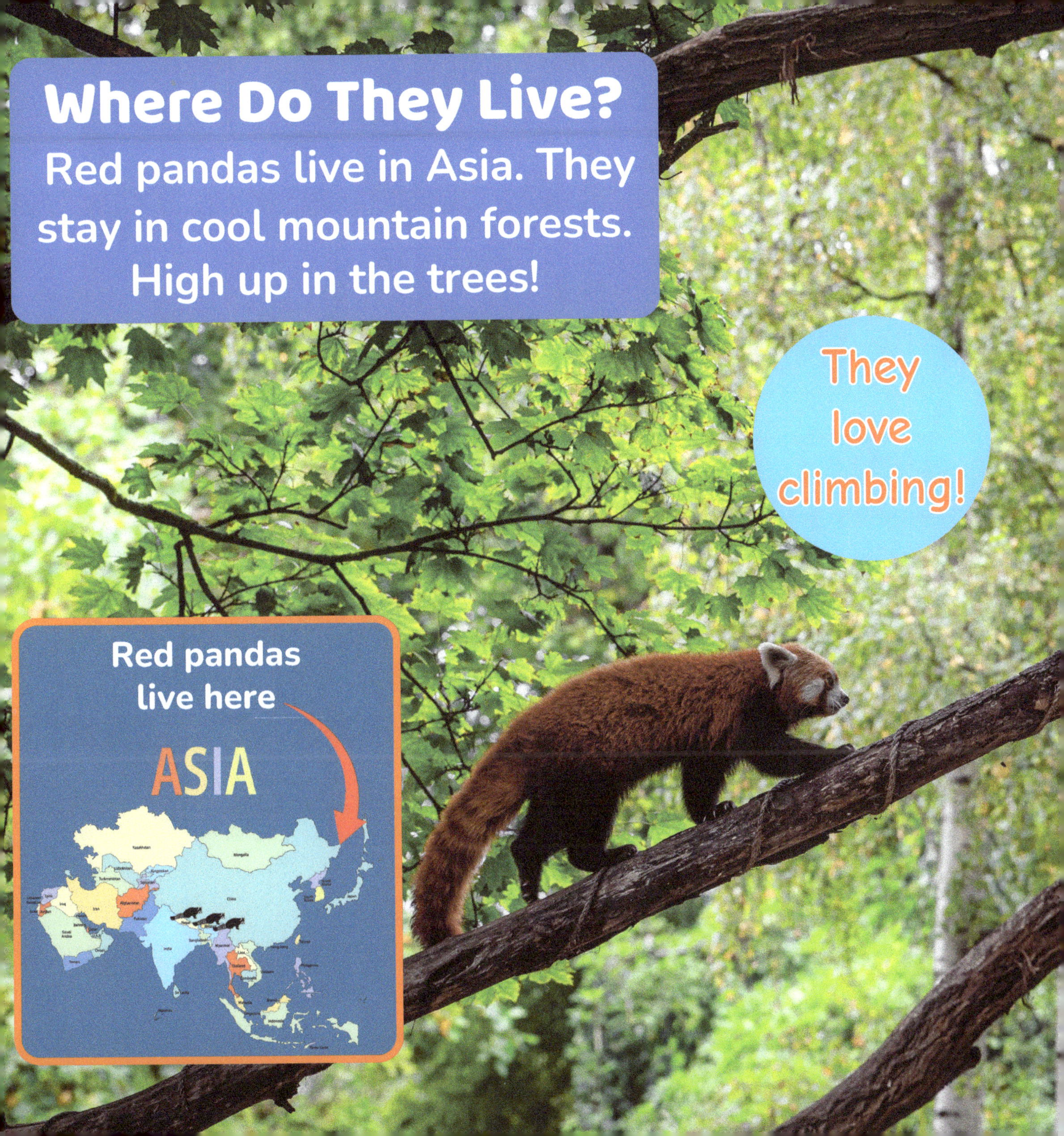

Where Do They Live?
Red pandas live in Asia. They stay in cool mountain forests. High up in the trees!
They love climbing!
Red pandas live here
ASIA

Red pandas love cool weather. They live high in the mountains where the air is crisp and cold.

Tree Climbers!
Red pandas love to climb.
Up, up, up — branch to
branch they go!

Balancing Act
Their long, bushy tails help them stay balanced on every branch.

Sharp Claws
Hold on Tight!
Red pandas have strong, curved claws. They grip the bark and hold on tight!

Snack Time
MUNCH
MUNCH
MUNCH
Red pandas love to eat bamboo.
They also munch on fruit and insects.

Sharp Teeth
Bamboo is tough — but not for red pandas! Their strong teeth crunch right through it.
CRUNCH!
CRUNCH!
CHOMP!

Quiet Animals

Red pandas are shy animals. They like quiet forests and tall trees.

Living Alone
Hello forest!
Most red pandas live alone. They explore the forest by themselves.

Baby Red Pandas

Red panda cubs grow slowly. Little by little, they learn to climb!

Talking

Red pandas make soft sounds. They squeak and chirp to say hello.

Squeak Squeak Chirp!

Watch Out!
Quick! This way!
Red pandas watch for danger in the forest. They hear a sound. Up the tree — fast!

Hide and Seek

Red pandas are good at hiding. Their fur helps them blend right into the trees.

Forest Friends
Red pandas share their forest with birds, monkeys, and squirrels. They all love life high in the trees!

Dawn and Dusk

Red pandas wake up at
dawn. They explore again
at dusk. They rest in the
quiet hours in between.

Nap Time
Red pandas nap in tree branches. They curl up in their fluffy tails. So soft. So still.
Zzzz...

Staying Warm
So cozy!
Red pandas wrap their tails around themselves when it's cold. Their fluffy tail is like a cozy blanket!

Nesting
I love my home!
Red pandas make nests in trees. Leaves and twigs make a cozy bed. They rest safe and high above the ground.

Needs Our Help

Red pandas are rare animals. There are not many left in the wild. Their forests are getting smaller.

Red Pandas and People
Protect!
Help!
Care!
Red pandas are wild animals. But people care about them. People work hard to protect their forest homes!

FUN FACT RECAP

 Red pandas love to eat bamboo.

 Red pandas live in mountain forests in Asia.

 Baby red pandas are called cubs.

 Red pandas use their tails to stay warm.

 Red pandas have striped tails and masked faces.

What We Learned

Red pandas are quiet, fluffy animals. They climb trees, eat bamboo, and curl up high in the cool mountain forest. They are a wonderful part of our world!

What was your favorite red panda fact?

QUIZ TIME

Can you remember what you learned about red pandas?

1. What do red pandas eat?

2. Where do they live?

3. What is a baby red panda called?

4. How do red pandas stay warm?

5. What sound do they make?

Words to Know

Bamboo — A plant that red pandas love to eat

Cub — A baby red panda

Forest — A place with many trees

Climb — To move up trees or other tall things

Tail — A long, furry part of the body used for balance

MORE AMAZING ANIMALS

Want to learn about more awesome animals?
Look for other books in the series!

Can you draw a red panda?
What would it be doing? Eating? Napping? Climbing?

Draw it here!